THE ALTERNATIVE TRUTH

by

Aaron Simmons Jr.

Dorrance Publishing Co
585 Alpha Drive
Pittsburgh, PA 15238
Visit our website at www.dorrancebookstore.com

ISBN: 979-8-88729-431-5
eISBN: 979-8-88729-931-0

CHAPTER I: A WORLD WITHOUT EMPATHY

It is past time to wake up, Brother John. We cannot sleep through what is happening in the year of 2019. The White Nationalist is in the White House. We must, every one of us, don the cloak of freedom. We must take upon ourselves the attitude of MARTIN LUTHER KING JUNIOR. Jim Crow is knocking at our door. He has come to make AMERICA great again. His tools are designed to strip us of our voting rights, and every gain that was earned by the blood of my brother; MEDGAR EVERS. Wake up, Brother John, you can't ride anymore. Now you must bear your own cross. Many songs have been sung, and many heroes have died, but still you have one foot in old Jim Crow's back door, while complaining about racial injustice. Are we our brother's keeper? Of course! Who the hell else?

I said that the self-proclaimed nationalist is in the NATION'S CAPITAL. His rhetoric is causing some people to lose their lives as the lady did in Charlottesville. He is making bigoted moves to reinstate the bigoted past. It is astonishing to see how popular his platform has become. LIFE, LIBERTY, AND THE PURSUIT OF HAPPINESS is to him: "FAKE NEWS!" What can be done? Voting isn't illegal yet, although laws are being passed to make it harder. Black women are voting dutifully. We must do likewise. We cannot give this would-be slave master four more years in the White House. Please bear with me, dear reader as my mind travels back to a time that is reminiscent of slavery.

The year was 1962. We were out of school for the summer, and as usual we worked on the farm during the summer months. A small crop duster biplane descended to within a few feet above our heads. Without warning the pilot released the poisonous DDT that was used in the early 1960s to kill insects. We ran out of the field but not before our lungs were filled with the now outlawed insecticide. This is a sample of what racism and slavery is capable of. Neither the pilot of the plane, nor the farmer whose crop was being dusted gave a rat's *** about the well-being of the people who were working in the field. Bigotry was just a matter of course in the year of 1962. The bigot in the White House intends to take us back in time to an era of JIM CROW LAWS. BIGOTRY is just a matter of course in the year 2019.

Dylan Roof, a White supremacist, murdered nine African Americans at a prayer service. He stated that his intent was to start a civil war. This egregious incident happened on June 17th, 2015. On October 2018 Robert D. Bowers entered a Jewish synagogue and killed eleven people while uttering anti-Semitic language. The lynching's of yesterday have been resurrected today. It is appalling—the PRESIDENT is lighting the fuse of discourse in our proud nation. Senseless murders such as these have been attributed to the callous and hateful rhetoric that flows from our nation's capital. Our bigoted bigot has waged war on those who have the courage to shed light on these injustices.

Pardoning racist terrorists, such as the sheriff of Arizona is but one example of his hateful intent. So please, Brother John, WAKE THE HELL UP! Indifference and self-pity are more deadly than the seven deadly sins where freedom is concerned. Someone said that freedom isn't free. The AMERICAN LIBRARY OF WAR CASUALTIES states that during the VIETNAM WAR, young Black males constituted 11 percent of our nation's population, but were dying in combat at 20 percent of all casualties during the early stages of conflict (Congress, 1965). This prompted then PRESIDENT LYNDON JOHNSON to reduce the number of Black men serving in VIETNAM.

We have been paying our dues to this nation, Brother John, but there are bigots who took the cowardly way out by dodging the draft. Now these same bigots are thumping their chest while advocating violence against our babies. If someone is offended by my rhetoric, then maybe they should take a long honest look at the 45th ADMINISTRATION'S MESSAGES OF DIVISION. His messages are promoting racism in AMERICA. The UNITED STATES CONSTITUTION a promise of unity and freedom. We pledge our allegiance to the Flag and we believed in freedom enough to put ourselves in harm's way, even though our fore-parents came here in chains.

Our heritage is rich. My father served during World War I. My older brother was in the Korean Conflict. I was in Vietnam. We only asked for empathy from a nation that has elected a WHITE NATIONALIST, as the most powerful leader in the world. What we got was a Super Bigot with an Authoritarian Ideology. Now let us examine the underlying intent of this Administration. One of its policies is: to ban people from this country who don't look as if they are from NORWAY. The utterings are again racist. It is an attempt to relegate us not only to the back of the bus, but also to the back of the employment line. We know about labeling. We are more labeled than commodities on a grocery store shelf. We have been called lazy and shiftless, while we built mansions for big fat bigots. Railroads were built from coast to coast by the sweat of our labor. From the cotton fields to the space program, we have carried our weight.

Even so, it never stopped the effort to dehumanize us. We must not fall asleep and misconstrue what is real and what is just <u>an alternative</u> <u>truth</u>. There is no empathy in presenting a blanket laden with small-pox to the indigenous people of AMERICA. Why kiss a rattlesnake? You know that his bite is poisonous. Beware, the super bigot has launched an attack upon anyone who is on a quest for freedom. The lesson is to wake the hell up. We are much more than the lies that were told about us. It is an insult to my intelligence, for someone to gauge my intelligence with dialogue that would attempt to relegate me to a position of subordination. There are those who say that we complain too much. My answer is *&#!@!/$%. Complaining is not the virus in this atrocious presentation of inhumane treatment. It is merely the symptoms of the dastardly deeds that have been perpetrated upon our people. You can't dog whistle me back into slavery!

CHAPTER 2: THE MISINFORMATION YEARS

I was sheltered and loved by my parents. They did their best to shelter me from this type of bigotry. They taught me to be upstanding, and honest, and strong. We were taught to help our neighbors and care for each other's children as our own. As a young boy, I soon learned that if you thought like that, then you would be ill-equipped for the challenges of today's world. Today's world is rife with hatred. I can remember the feelings of discomfort, when I got old enough to read the signs that were posted in public places such as "White Only." It was a feeling not unlike the feelings a person gets when they need to apologize for hurting someone's feelings, or feeling unworthy to belong to a first-class group of people.

I also noted that Black people acted subservient around White people, because that was the JIM CROW LAW. If they didn't they could be killed. I was innocent and naïve. I was asleep to the real intent of those who would enslave me. I was as a person to whom someone had slipped some drug called <u>misinformation</u> into my drink, a drug that would cause me to believe lies about who I was. The drug called misinformation, presented me with lies that depicted my subordinate station in life as opposed to the special privileges that White people enjoyed. It seemed that in my slumber-like state, I was always dragging around a heavy weight. However, all weight lifters know that weights can be used for conditioning.

I only knew that there was a lot that I didn't know. For instance, why Black people had to always ride in the back of the transit bus. I wondered how all of the children that rode on our school bus could fit in this small space. I also wondered why the farmer, whom we worked for, sometimes talked in a loud tone of voice as if we all had hearing problems. I noticed that his conversations with White folks were spoken in normal tones. This practice was just one of the dehumanizing tactics that were intended to give us the lying concept: that we were inferior to Whites. The farmer called his dog in a loud voice also.

I developed a determination that I would never let someone dictate a lie to me about any part of me that is less than I know about who I am. If my positive air or self-esteem, conflicts with a condition of employment, then I may be on the wrong job. I strive to be amiable with most people, but the world is full of snakes. Wake up, Brother John, and stop walking around bowing, and shuffling and acting like a damn fool, even though you know that you're not, but all for the sake of trying to please a sadistic son of a bigot! Here is an excerpt from STEPHEN FOSTERS song "Old Black Joe."

"Gone are the days when my heart was young and gay, gone are my friends from the cotton fields away, gone from the earth to a better land I know, I hear the gentle voices calling, OLD BLACK JOE." SEPHEN FOSTER wrote "Old Black Joe" in the year of 1860. (Foster 1865) The Civil War was being fought over slavery.

AFRICAN AMERICANS, SUCH AS OLD BLACK JOE WERE BEING LYNCHED OR BEATEN TO WITHIN AN INCH OF THEIR LIVES! YES, SIR, THE SLAVE-OWNERS WOULD TRY TO TAKE THE HIDE RIGHT OFF OF YOUR ASS. OLD BLACK JOE COULD HAVE BEEN REMEMBERED LIKE MAYBE, OLD YELLER DOG, OR SOME OTHER OBEDIENT BEAST OF BURDEN, BUT NOT AS ANOTHER HUMAN BEING. THE SLAVES WERE NOT TREATED WITH ANYTHING RESEMBLING GENTLE VOICES, OR GENTLE ANY DAMN THING. STEPHEN, THIS IS A BOGUS ALTERNATIVE TRUTH.

There is an AMERICAN however, who abstained from the slave ideology. MARK TWAIN is considered one of White America's greatest writers, and he railed against slavery with literary novels and letters to gain his point. The famous novel, *The Adventures of Huckleberry Finn* is a depiction of a thirteen-year-old White kid trying to help a Black slave run away to freedom on a makeshift raft. In the story the Black man is known as <u>NIGGER-JIM.</u> We soon learn that Jim gains his freedom. Such was the storytelling genius of this literary Abolitionist. If the slave-catchers had caught Jim and Huck, it would have been like: "Damn! Old Nigger-Jim stole more chain than he could carry! Cheers for Mark Twain." Anyone who has an ounce more compassion for a Black citizen, than they do for a dog should be commended.

CHAPTER 3: RECONSTRUCTING OLD JIM CROW

The dictionary defines bigotry as being prejudiced toward a person, or people, based on their membership of a particular group. My definition of a super bigot is a person or people who uses the power of a position of authority to commit acts of bigotry. I am looking at the policies of this Administration. These policies are reeking of the White Nationalist Ideology. Here is the vehicle and chauffeur that are moving these policies. The counsel to the President brings to the table: a ban on Muslims, or people from Muslim countries. There is also a concerted effort to disregard the provisions of the UNITED STATES CONSTITUTION—in which all of our CIVIL RIGHTS ARE GUARANTEED. With the weakening of the Constitution there would be a Nationalist movement to fill the void. Nationalism is a concept of a country, wherein a single group, or race of people are the only ones with economic and political power. This concept is driven by the fear that a concerted effort is being made to promote genocide of the White race.

This preposterous lie is designed to garner angst among innocent White citizens. Another carefully thought-out plan is to load the Federal benches with far-right conservative judges. The provisions of the constitution could then be interpreted from a perspective that would promote the policies of the White Nationalist President. White Nationalist, White Supremacist, Ku Klux Klan, Nazi Party, all have the White superior, but the title: White Nationalist, as proclaimed by our 45th President shows a not-so-sinister face to the nation. History teaches us that the first Constitutional right to be attacked by an authoritarian system of Government is freedom of the press. This Democratic right is then replaced by a misinformation campaign, that would be designed to promote the policies of an authoritarian regime.

A constant slogan that is being heard from this 45th Administration is "Fake News." It is meant to confuse the public concerning what is real news and what is an Alternative Truth. Other consequences of the threat to the Constitution are Civil Rights gains such as: the Affirmative Action Program. Voting Rights are in the crosshairs of this Nationalist agenda, as well as the Roe v. Wade Victory for Women's Rights to Pro-Choice. If left un-checked even Chattel Slavery could rear its ugly head under this onslaught of Jim-Crow policies. The White House strategist is no longer in the White House, but the racist seeds that he planted while there, has sprouted into a very bad apple tree. Now we have a right-wing would-be Authoritarian President with a nationalist ideology, who is embracing the policies of a known dictator from Russia.

Pardoning racist torturers and defying the courts, while appointing an Attorney General as his personal attorney, are an indications of moving toward an Authoritarian system of Government. It would be like Nazi USA. Someone has perhaps bumped their head on that idea. Why would right-thinking and freedom-loving people, allow this great country of ours, to be an Authoritarian stronghold? Daybreak is here, and we all must wake up! Freedom is as fleeting as money. If you don't go to work, then you won't get paid. Let's go to work at the polls, and vote against "Old Jim Crow." The Senate far-right Republicans seem to be intimidated by the 45-caliber Administration. Then misinformation issuing from the White House has garnered support from super bigots, little bigots, and racist want-to-be bigots.

It was a grand, and grave scheme for the would-be dictator to march toward the election. The reasoning is that: the reelection of some congressmen, could be compromised with a negative review from the 45th Administration, thereby short-circuiting their careers. This caving gives lie to the promise to uphold the UNITED STATES CONSTITUTION. THOUSANDS OF SOLDIERS HAVE DIED. I have met some of the bravest, and most honorable people of more than one race during my stint in the military, and other walks of life. White people have given their lives during the struggle for our freedom. Many of them have raised their voices against injustices toward our people. I thank them, with great appreciation, for their valiant efforts. These people, I believe have genuine concern for the cohesion, and strength of our nation.

Meanwhile, there are those, who would work toward dividing this nation with the ideology of a Nationalistic and Fascist type of GOVERNMENT. So now we have an anomaly. We have a Republican Party that has been consumed by the Nationalist, in a fashion, that is not unlike a giant amoeba devouring a helpless paramecium. What is appalling to me is their willingness to cave to Old Jim Crow.

CHAPTER 4: THE PANDEMIC

In the year 2020, a pandemic has gripped the world with a devastating effect upon the population. It started in the month of February, and by July of that year, it had claimed the lives of over 140,000 people in the United States. As usual Black Americans were dying at a faster rate than White Americans. The institutional explanation was: we don't eat healthy food, we don't exercise enough, and we can't afford health insurance. The truth of it all is blowing in the wind. Meanwhile the 45[Th] Administration is downplaying the serious effects of the virus. As the death toll climbed, some states were forced to store bodies in refrigerated trucks. The bodies that were not claimed within a certain amount of time were buried in mass graves. There were rumors that White patients were given preference over Black patients, with the breathing machines. The 45th Administration claimed it to be a Democratic Hoax.

During this period, certain statements from the White House were confusing, such as real men didn't have to wear masks. I believe that this radical statement caused many to scoff at the idea of a pandemic. There were also statements coming from the administration such as: the virus will disappear, and bleach could be injected into the body to cure the virus infection. The statements may have been uttered in an attempt at humor, but people were still dying in record numbers from the virus. I entertained a dreadful thought. If Black people were dying at a much greater rate than others, then would the idea surface to commit mass genocide on them? This is how I viewed the contents of the 45's character.

During this time the whole world watched in horror as Derek Chauvin, a police officer, knelt upon George Floyd's neck for nearly nine minutes. We could not believe that George Floyd was being lynched on national television. It is now history. Protests and riots broke out on a global scale. Federal Law Enforcement Officers were stationed in the cities, across America. I likened it to a kind of Armageddon. I gleaned this thought from the hateful rhetoric, that was coming from the White House. In my idea an oppressed people need concrete solutions to their problems. With no hope in sight, then panic will fill the void. The White Nationalist ideology was coloring my reasoning. I paid strict attention to the voice of this leader of the free world. My thoughts were that he lacked leadership when a calm voice of assurance was needed. There was only ridicule.

The President issued a statement that I will now paraphrase. "Old George Floyd is smiling down at the good fortune we are having with our economy. I shuddered to think of four more years under this bigoted administration. It had shown total disregard for the emotional agony of George Floyd's family. This Administration was showing encouragement to the rogue cops that were killing Black people. On August 28th the bigoted 45 held a rally. At that rally the crowd was told that: "protesters were nothing more than thugs, who didn't even know George Floyd." This country won its Independence, while protesting the unfair treatment, that they were receiving from England. To not protest would be to accept whatever future that bigots, and the like would design for us. Therefore we need to vote now or face a scary four more years with this KU KLUX KLAN AMINISTRATION.

His agenda is set against people of color, and I would venture that it's not even in the best interest of the country, but in his own interest. If a person of color is killed by a rogue cop unjustly, then the people will protest. The President then exercises his vise grip of oppression by pretending that the act of protesting is a crime. He rallies his base around this, disregard for the first amendment to our UNITED STATES CONSTITUTION. It doesn't seem to matter to him how many lives are lost. The protesters are dehumanized by being labeled as thugs. If this lie passes muster, then it is easier to oppress them. They can then be treated with the kind of inhumane tactics that were used at the southern border. As for tearing the country apart, isn't that the idea? Meanwhile, Derek Chauvin was very comfortable as he knelt upon George Floyd's neck. He seemed composed as he adjusted his knee. He must have felt the vertebrae column, and he had to know when Mr. Floyd took his last breath.

The image is etched in my psyche as a monument to the cost of being Black in America. George Floyd was senselessly, and cruelly murdered in America while millions watched. Meanwhile the bigoted bigot, by way of Twitter, continued to reach down and stoke the Fascist flames of bigotry, that burned beneath a seething cauldron of racist rhetoric. The pandemic still raged on with the same indifference, as it killed Black Americans discriminately.

CHAPTER 5: THE OPPRESIVE REGIME

An effort toward a return to the Jim Crow era, should remind us that our work has just begun. We have bravely endured, all manner of inhumane treatment, such as lynching, drug infestations, Jim Crow laws against Voting Rights and "last hired, first fired" practices in the workplace. Even the Government got in on the act with: "The Tuskegee Experiment." (USPHS, 1932–1972). We are in no way tired. We were made to endure. We recognize that the Nationalist are launching a campaign to divide the world. Bigots are designing a movement to resurrect a Hitler-like society. The 45th Administration is testing the water, by hinting at eight more years as president.

Meanwhile, we have a far-right Senate, that is led by an opponent of any program, that would oppose the policies of the 45. The actions, or inactions of this Congress can be volatile toward the stability of the UNITED STATES CONSTITUTION. Right now the action of this Congress is to dance to the orchestration of the Executive branch of the Government. The inaction is not legislating laws that would counteract the erosion of Civil Rights. Our future and our children's future hang in the balance. I rest my conviction on section 2 of the 15th amendment to the Constitution, which gives Congress the power to legislate laws, that could be counter to voter suppression. We cannot afford to ignore this thrust toward our mass genocide.

If we don't have a voice at the ballot box, we then will face a dark future under this Administration. This is not "Fake News!" It has been noted that some parasites can apply an anesthesia while lunching on their prey. The victim does not feel any pain and believes that all is normal. So have some voters have been lulled to the concept that locking up babies is a normal AMERICAN-LIKE ideology. It seems to be more Hitleresque, for as I write these words, there is an encampment that is not unlike a concentration camp. In it are 300 children. Their ages range from infant to seventeen. There are reports that, they have no toothpaste, diapers, and other toiletries that are essential for decent bodily care. The place where they are housed was designed for 104 people—yet there are 300 hungry children, who are sleeping on a concrete floor, and living in atrocious conditions. The place where they are held captive is not Nazi, Germany. It is a place in America—land of the free, and home of the brave. "Der Fuhrer," who is in charge, is not Adolf Hitler. "Der Fuhrer is "THE SUPER BIGOT."

Studies reveal a right-wing theory that is being floated among White voters. It is called: THE GREAT REPLACEMENT THEORY. This theory is a misinformation tactic, that proclaim: White people are to be replaced by minorities, and illegal immigrants. This tactic has been used time and again to accuse someone of a misdeed and then commit the infraction themselves. I point to a novel by WILLIAM LUTHER PIERCE, known as the *Turner Diaries*. The *Turner Diaries* advocates mass genocide against minorities. William Luther Pierce was the head of The National Alliance, a Neo-Nazi Group. We cannot continue to ignore these efforts to neutralize our importance as citizens with rights, as promised by the Constitution.

Take a hard look at the reality of the situation. Those old "YES, SIR BOSS," cooning slogans won't get you by anymore. The racist-right wants you dead, or in the privatized prison system, which is just an alternative to Chattel Slavery. This movement is not to be ignored as more Right-Wing Politicians are embracing the call for Christian White Nationalism. This is the same Ku Klux Klan soup being warmed up. This movement is sweeping the country. It means that they are the only group of people who are privileged in America.

Here is where we can survive this racist movement. MARCUS Garvey believed, that we could thrive and prosper, if we could find the cohesion, to spend our money in trade with each other. His plan was successful. Subsequently he was banished from

America. I understand that the charges against him were trumped up. Even though he had to leave the country, the seeds of prosperity had been sown into the hearts and minds of many people. We should accept the idea of not living on crumbs, from a trickle-down, racist doctrine. We should come together as every other group has done. Some of us are skilled at surfing the market and landing Federal contracts for our businesses. It is what we should be doing. That skill is not for everyone.

I am proud to see our young men majoring in skills such as Electrical Engineering, and other enriching tools that will be needed in the future. Civil rights initiatives have opened the door for many of us. When the White House declared a shutdown, because of the pandemic, the Administration indicated, that the ones most hurt by the shutdown were Democrats. The UNITED STATES CHAMBER OF SMALL BUSINESS, representing roughly 240,000 Black businesses nationally, stated that, "the Government shutdown, obstructs Black entrepreneurships. We must not put all of our eggs in one basket. To reiterate, we must come together as never before against this MAGA, dog-whistle, slavery ideology.

As I mentioned earlier, illicit drugs are our enemy! THE INTERNATIONAL CENTER FOR PRISON STUDIES, STATES THAT: "People of color experience dis-crimination at every stage of the judicial system, and are more likely to be stopped, searched, arrested, and convicted. They are harshly sentenced, and then saddled with a lifelong criminal record. This is particularly the case for drug convictions." Crack is a drug that has been devastating to the Black community. Hundreds of thousands of our young people are incarcerated each year, while their White counterparts go free. To smoke crack is a sickness for Black addicts, but is viewed by the courts as a crime, worthy of harsh penalties under the law.

A new drug epidemic hit the American public, around the year 1999. THE DELPHI BEHAVIORAL GROUP has some startling statistics. In that year, pharmaceutical companies assured the communities that, opioids were safe as pain relievers. An average of 115 Americans were dying each day from opioid-related overdose. Government treatment facilities, provided care under the direction of THE SUBSTANCE ABUSE AND MENTAL HEALTH ADMINISTRATION. While this is commendable, one can't ignore the lost generation of our young Black Americans, who were treated as criminals instead of addicted human beings.

AARON SIMMONS JR.

He who has eyes let him see. The only way out for you, if you try crack or other unlawful drugs, is prison or death! No one gave a damn if you were on drugs. It was when White people started dying from drug overdose that drug addiction suddenly became an illness instead of a crime. It is still a crime for Black drug addicts. So, wake the hell up!

CHAPTER 6: THE RIGHT-WING CONSERVATIVE MACHINE

Let us look at the GOP RIGHT-WING CONSERVATIVE MACHINE. In order to shed light on our current Jim Crow-like far right-wing conservative dilemma, we must take a closer look at some components of the GOP MACHINE. I have placed them in the order that I perceive to be a starting point. They are: The Federalist society, The Honest Elections Project, and The American Center for Voting Rights. Intertwined with the Federalist Society is The UNITED STATES SUPREME COURT, as well as other lower Federal courts. The Federalist Society began in the 1980s. It started with a group of students from The University of Chicago, and Yale University. (Some have credited Harvard). The Federalist Society is known for supplying right-wing conservative Presidents with Justices, that share they're conservative ideologies We now have a six-justice majority on the Supreme court.

They are: CHIEF JUSTICE JOHN ROBERT, SAMUEL ALITO, CLARENCE THOMAS, who has been called by the Federalist Society as the closest thing to a pure Federalist Society Judge. (I suspect that there may be other labels by some observers). President Donald Trump Appointed NEIL GORSUCH, BRETT CAVANAUGH, AND AMY CONEY BARETT. All of these conservative Justices were supplied by The Federalist Society. It would be fair to say that these Supreme Court Justices do not have an apolitical agenda as evidenced by the far-right conservative-oriented decisions that are being issued from the SCOTUS. They have been accused of overreaching, as in their decision to overturn Roe. This decision was in direct alignment with the conservative ideology of the conservative Republican agenda.

While it has been found that the majority of the voters do not support this decision, to overturn Roe, this court is only tuned to the wishes of its masters, (The Federalist Society.) I will revisit the super majority Supreme Court later in this chapter. The Honest Election Project aka HEP, is at the forefront of voter suppression. They present a direct challenge to the voting rights act. They are a dark-money group that threatens our elections. Leonard Leo, who is Vice President of the Federalist Society, restructured a fifteen-year-old conservative nonprofit to create HEP. HEP has a history of donations to conservative causes, and has been tied to National Republican Organizations. HEP has been known to spread voter-fraud disinformation. They have funded groups that waged disinformation attacks.

The American Center for Voting Rights is a precursor to HEP. Some of their tactics include, prosecuting voter fraud. They support voter suppression laws and media campaigns toward voter suppression. Elections experts called the HEP a voter suppression business, of wholly debunked conspiracy theories, and election meddling that endangers our democracy. The State of Florida now has an elections police unit. With the SCOTUS filled with the required number of justices, dark money is now aimed toward the Voter Suppression activity.

At this time I would like to commend MISS SHERILYN IFILL, who is a law professor, and past President, and Director-Counsel of the NAACP DEFENSE FUND. She has been committed to the cause of minority voting rights. She has stated that: "Black women voters have proved incredibly resilient, leading record turnouts, for the Democratic Base in the 2020 Elections, and in the Georgia Special Elections in 2021. Black voters stood in line for over nine hours in Fulton County, Georgia in the 2020 Presidential Primaries, during some of the worst days of the pandemic. Their patriotism, and determination were rewarded by the Republican Party with a new set of voter suppression laws, including one section that criminalizes giving water to voters standing in line."

Meanwhile, The Federalist Society has been successful in placing people in strategic positions, such as the conservative majority in the SCOTUS. This majority seems to serve with unwavering faithfulness, the right-wing conservative constituency that placed them there. The shadow docket is being used in an unusual fashion by this conservative coalition of jurors and have become a tool that's used to overturn stalwart, court opinions, that had been respected, under the regal mantle of, "Stare Decisis." These decisions have become guidelines in jurisprudence for future cases. This conservative majority is chipping away at such cases as Roe vs. Wade with the Shadow Docket, and sometimes the decision is written on a single sheet of paper.

The Shadow Docket has a history of being used for emergency cases such as the death penalty. This conservative majority is disregarding Oral Arguments, and briefs from lower courts, concerning cases that have been appealed to The Supreme Court. Complaints have been lodged by concerned citizens that the Court's decisions have been murky, and too ambiguous to be used as guidelines for the lower courts to follow. Here is a case that exemplifies the attitude of the conservative majority on the Supreme Court.

This SCOTUS decision involves David Ramirez, and Barry Lee Jones, who is on death row in the State of Arizona. Their lawyers were inept. They argued to the point that their Sixth Amendment Rights under the UNITED STATES CONSTITUTION were violated. (The Right to Adequate Counsel). Ramirez said that his counsel failed to investigate his intellectual disability, and Jones said that his lawyer ignored evidence, that Jones may have been innocent of the crime that he was charged with. In 2017 a Federal judge overturned Jones's conviction and offered the state a choice of retrying Jones or releasing him. The State of Arizona appealed the case to the Supreme Court. The Court upheld The State's decision. Writing for the majority, JUSTICE CLARENCE THOMAS, explained the Court's decision thusly: "In our Dual-Sovereign system, Federal Courts must afford unwavering respect to the centrality, of a trial of a criminal case in state court." "Wainwright 433 US AT 90." That is the moment at which Society's resources have been concentrated. In order to decide, within the limits of human fallibility, the question of guilt or innocence of one of its citizens." IBID, I see Collins 506 US, {OP SLIP AT 8}. "Such an intervention is also an affront to the State and its citizens, who have rendered a verdict of guilty after considering all of the evidence before them. Federal Courts years later lack the competence and authority to re-litigate a State's criminal case.

JUSTICE SOTOMEYER wrote in dissent: "THIS DECISION IS PERVERSE,"… And so goes the machinery of the far-right conservative GOP. Alternative System. The Court seems to serve the conservative body, even to the point of, disregarding the precedents that are set in stone such as STARE DECISIS. The Shadow Docket has become standard procedure, and is seemingly, used by the SCOTUS to skirt the historical briefs, and appeals from the lower courts. Open and transparent arguments are a near forgotten procedure as accusations have been made of decisions being made under a cloak of secrecy, with the aforementioned one page of a non-sensical answer presented to the public.

In the above case the SCOTUS seemed to place a lower court decision in a position of uncontested power even over itself. The ordinary citizen has not a chance with this conservative majority hand-picked Court against the State, regardless of the evidence in their favor. The Sixth Amendment, in my opinion was trounced by the SCOTUS IN THE ABOVE CASE. The SCOTUS seemingly applied the tenth amendment to the case in point, which states that: When a question is not enumerated in the US CONSTITUTION, then that decision would belong to the people. The people in this context meaning the States. What is precarious about this type of Textualist, and originalist, method of reasoning is, it seems to render an upside-down application of the Tenth Amendment clause, with its ambiguous interpretation. I am seeing this decision as in the application of the Sixth Amendment. The lower court judge had it right, because of the "adequate counsel" enumeration in the Constitution.

This far-right conservative majority is scary as hell, because they are not apolitical. Their textualist approach to interpreting the law seem to me to bend to the will of their far-right constituents. Some of the framers of the constitution were slaveowners. Would this far-right super majority apply the textualist method to deciding a question of slavery, if the question came before them? I ask this question because to apply the textualist method would be to interpret the Constitution, exactly as it was written by the framers. At least this is what the conservative justices are proclaiming. With no favorable enumeration, against the ownership of slaves in the original text of the US Constitution, until the thirteenth Amendment to the Constitution, would they then, relegate authority to the people, (States), under the Tenth Amendment to decide the question of slavery?

JAMES MADISON, who owned over one hundred slaves in the early 1800s, and thirty-six slaves around 1830, died without setting them free. History tells us, that he worked them from sunup until sundown for six days a week. History has tried to paint JAMES MADISON as a humane person who was against slavery. He was the foremost architect of the, UNITED STATES CONSTITUTION-yet he owned over one hundred slaves. Furthermore, he sired a son, whose name was JIM. JIM'S mother was a Black slave woman, who was JAMES MADISON'S property. Sadly, with Jim being of a Black mother, he was also a slave, and was sold when he was a teenager. Would James Madison then be a role model for a textualist-oriented decision to revisit The Thirteenth Amendment?

Would CLARENCE THOMAS WRITE THE OPINION FOR THE MAJORITY? Although the Thirteenth Amendment seems to be a stalwart barrier against chattel slavery in the UNITED STATES, this far-right majority SCOTUS, can find a way to give preference to the States, over Constitutional rights. For example they ignored a STARE DECISIS-laden, monumental decision by allowing the State of Texas to legislate a law, which was in direct opposition to ROE VS WADE. ROE was a Constitutional right at the time, that Texas enacted a law that gives the ordinary citizen, consent to collect a bounty of 10,000 dollars from abortion providers for performing an abortion. It sounds preposterous, but this is the SCOTUS, that we are trusting in the year 2020.

Calls are for the expansion of the Court. The right to vote under the Fifteenth Amendment was actually the first-time color and race was enumerated in the UNITED STATES CONSTITUTION, and only then, for the purpose of helping White people decide how to count slaves in the process of determining the outcome of elections, and apply taxes. A slave in the year 1857, which was nearly one hundred years after the ratification of the constitution was seen as three-fifths of a White person. Would the present-day SCOTUS apply textualism in this context with this super majority? Could the SCOTUS, now decide that the dreaded, Dred Scott Decision was the right call after all? Known as the worst decision in Supreme Court history, the Supreme Court held in 1856 that: persons of African descent cannot be and were never intended to be citizens under the US Constitution. To quote the decision: "The plaintiff is without standing to file a suit." It was the ratification of the Thirteenth, and fourteenth Amendments to the Constitution, after the civil war, wherein the Dred Scott decision was superseded. It was a far-right Court then, and it is a far-right Court in 2020. It also may sound far-fetched to some, but it sounds far-right to me.

Remember that there are laws enacted by some States, that are intended to make the mention of slavery a crime, within our schools. The idea is to prevent White people's children from thinking them to be bad people. If that Jim Crow law can fly in the face of the First Amendment, then how much more can be chipped away from our freedom. I believe that it is time to expand the Supreme Court. To wait until after the midterm elections would be a fatal mistake. We have the House and the Presidency now, so let us work toward ending the Filibuster Rule. We should be about the business of saving the future of our children while we have a chance.

CHAPTER 7: FIENDS FROM HELL

MUCH HAS HAPPENED IN THE YEAR 2021. THE pandemic has receded. I give the credit to the CDC, and DR. FAUCI. The 45 lost the election to PRESIDENT JOE BIDEN, a former VICE PRESIDENT. The 45 held that the election was invalid and is holding to this stupid assertion unto this day. The threat upon civil rights gains seem more imminent now with a seemingly insurmountable source of far-right dark money flowing freely to the coffers of the oppression-oriented, far-right conservative political apparatus. Individual states are passing laws that can overturn landmark court decisions. Civil Rights laws are beginning to fall, as I predicted, and the midterm elections are on the horizon.

The economy is reeling from the effects of the pandemic. As the country struggles through these uncertain times, I am always looking at periods in our history to draw a measure of solace from, as a person in the desert would search for an oasis of water. We are in need of a political oasis. We don't need racist assassins seeking immortality at the expense of innocent citizens. From the year 1962, we learned that a crop duster, and a farmer felt totally within their rights to treat people of color with the nonchalant disdain in which they viewed us.

To offer an example of this disdain, I present the following regretful analogy.... The sun shone brightly in the Mississippi sky, giving life to the sweet petunias that grew in the rich Southern soil. A boy-child as innocent as the flowers and filled with the hope and aspirations and whatever dreams that a child may dream was also filled with an exuberance of life. In his boy-child's world, he would have no fear of the monsters that would soon advance upon him, as a hungry lion would advance upon an unsuspecting gazelle. They tortured him for what must have seemed like an eternity before he gave up the gift of life.

A flower had been clipped from the garden before the bloom could open. The boy-child was in the clutches of fiends worthy of hell. They were not as merciful as the lion, for the lion would swiftly dispatch the gazelle, and that for food. The monsters would torture their victim, as an ideological cause that White Supremacy must be known. Sadistically they tortured their prey, and this with an insane mindset for no sane person would mutilate a child in this fashion. They were exonerated by a jury of their peers. As the lion would finish his meal, so did the monsters from old MISSISSIPPI dispose of the boy-child's body.... As a Mississippi mom presented fresh cut flowers to her inner circle of friends, MAMIE TILL prepared to show her once beautiful boy-child to the world.

There is no oasis visible on the political horizon. There is only an effort to reiterate the fiend-like deeds of the past and this by fiend-like creatures of the present. As mentioned earlier, States are passing laws that are reminiscent of codes that were established during the early periods of Reconstruction. These codes were called: "BLACK CODES," AND THEY WERE ESTABLISHED TO ENHANCE VOTER SUPPRESSION. These Black Codes also enforced segregation. They were later adopted into what became: THE JIM CROW LAWS, of the Southern States. They were legislated by the Southern States that were beginning to organize State Governments after the Civil War.

The State of Mississippi held the more egregious codes against freedmen, as ex-slaves were labeled by the Federal Government at that time. The State of South Carolina had a more enumerated set of Black Codes, but they were no less egregious. Now in the year 2022, as the midterm elections approach, there are unfounded allegations of voter fraud, and it is being used to fuel these Jim Crow laws again with the intent of suppressing the voting rights of Black citizens. People are seeking office, and leaning on endorsements from a far-right Nationalist, who has authoritarian plans for America. I see endorsements of this kind, made to people whose popularity stems from their athletic abilities. I warn that we must be diligent and wary, lest we are unknowingly fattening up frogs for snakes. We are trying to understand these "Alternative Truths." If Roe can be overturned, because it is not enumerated in the UNITED STATES CONSTITUTION, will the 1964 Civil Rights act follow a similar fate? These Alternative Truths can become law if we don't weed out our would-be slave masters. The creed of America, though is for the ones who reach out and grasp it. We have paid for it with our blood, sweat, and tears. Therefore, the application of financial freedom, through cohesive business decisions would be balm against the pain that's inflicted by the many fiend-like that are looking to take us down into a poverty-ridden hell.

At this time I would like to honor some of our most recent martyrs. They are: SANDRA BLAND, TAMIR RICE, TRAVON MARTIN, MICHAEL BROWN, JOHN CRAWFORD, EZELL FORD, DANTE PARKER, ERIC GARNER, DANTE PARKER, TINISHA ANDERSON, AKAI GURLEY, MARTIN LEE ANDERSON, GEORGE FLOYD, AND BREONNA TAYLER. This list is incomplete. The whole world knows about the history of the BLACK AMERICAN EXPERIENCE. It is ingrained in the fabric of our culture. There is a giant effort to distort this truth in the minds of our youth. The fabled Hercules would shy away from such a daunting task. I view it as an "in your face" tactic, from a far-right political strategist. Salt when applied to an open wound can be excruciating. The effort to keep our youth from the truth is futile because "his truth is marching on." The effort to suppress it on serves to promote the reality of the Black experience in AMERICA. The history of the martyrs that are listed above cannot be legislated away.

CHAPTER 8: SYSTEMIC VOTER SUPPRESSION

As I have stated, the world full of snakes and things. Politicians are power-mad in the year 2022, with the resurrected "WHITE NATIONALIST IDEOLOGY." Someone said that history repeats itself. Indeed, it seems that the period of reconstruction has returned, like a déjà vu phenomenon. It was during this period that the KU Klux Klan was formed. Someone seems to be realizing that we are not oppressed enough and are doing their part to fix that imagined oversight. It seems that the idea surfaced that States could overturn a national Presidential election if enough crooks were involved. Freedom is hanging in the balance henceforth. A civil war could ensue if this country is not strong enough to rein in a far-right Federal court system with its conservative judges, and openly bigoted State Governors who place political success above the welfare of <u>all</u> of its citizens.

"The Big Lie," is now being unraveled, but is in no way being weakened, as the desire for power is a trump card over the desire for integrity. What is being offered by politicians is a kind of "Alternative Truth," to an apathetic and weary society. We must not be so complacent that we accept these blatant misconceptions. The pandemic and inflation, have shaken this Nation's citizens to the core of their souls. The Republicans are finding low-hanging fruit for their platforms against the present political party in such a calamity of events. The midterm elections have begun.

The date is June 24th. This day is important because, the far-right majority of the SCOTUS voted to overturn ROE, which was a landmark decision in the year 1973, and which had withstood the challenge by, CASEY VS Roe in 1992. A Federal Judge has blocked parts of the State of Florida's Voter Suppression Law for now. (LARGE, APRIL 2022). I said for now! A lot of energy and money is being spent on racist policies, (aka cultural differences), in America. As I mentioned earlier, an elections police unit has been formed by the State of Florida. This is a far-right JIM CROW-laden move that is geared to suppress the minority vote. Equally egregious is: election officials in the states are being replaced by election deniers with officials, who share their political beliefs, such as so-called pro-life ideologies, and other far-right sympathies. It is like having the fox in charge of the hen house.

SUMMARY

In summary I am reminded, that the coldhearted attitude of the farmer and the crop duster was my orientation to bigotry in America. To further the realization that we are hanging by a thread, is the nonchalance with which our plight as an oppressed people is viewed with delight by the oppressors. The word "woke," which is used as a wake-up call by our Black leaders to call attention to racial injustices, is now being used in a pejorative manner by the oppressors, to mock our quest for respect and dignity as AMERICAN CITIZENS. An enormous amount of time and money is being spent to maintain that oppression. The Federalist Society, from where far-right judges are chosen has the power through the judge-picking process to shape the future of American politics, and therefore the future of American citizen by virtue of the interpretation of the UNITED STATES CONSTITUTION.

The political party that controls Congress after the midterm elections can legislate our way out of this calamity, but a Far-right Congress has failed to admonish a would-be dictator who has come to town as a Carpetbagger, with a satchel full with "ALTERNATIVE TRUTHS." We do not get Reparations, but we do get racist cops, who are supported by bigots. The racists are working to kill our people in a fashion not unlike they're fore-parents did during Reconstruction. The Reparation money is probably being spent on a nationwide effort to save the Monarch Butterfly. We have the Christian White Nationalist movement whose aim is to shape politics and pass laws that reflect only their views of Christianity, thus changing everyone's view of what life will be in America. I HOPE TO SEE YOU AT THE POLLS!

9 798888 729431 5